@

@

@

@

@

@

@

@

@

@

@

@

@

@

@

@

@

@

@

@

@

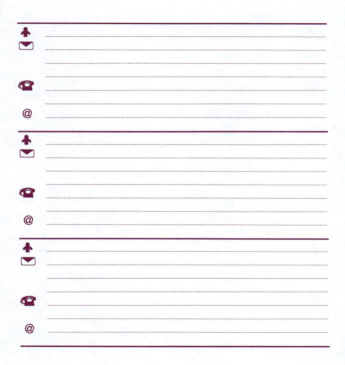

@

@

@

@

@

@

@

@

@

@

@

@

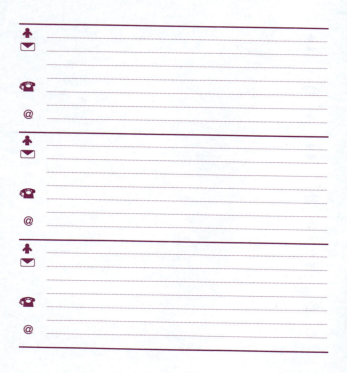

@

@

@

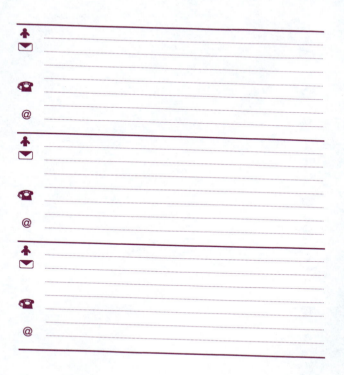

d

@

@

@

d

@

@

@

@

@

@

d

@

@

@

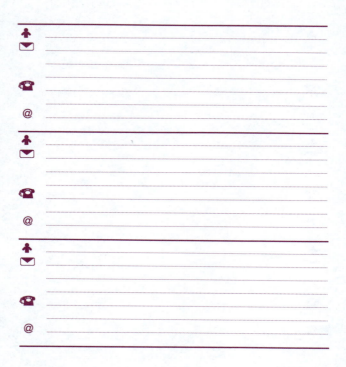

@

@

@

@

@

@

@

@

@

@

@

@

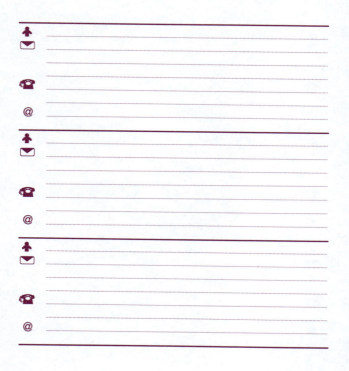

@

@

@

f

@

@

@

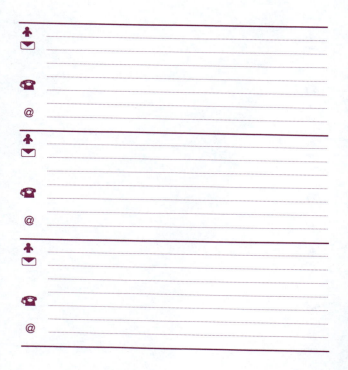

f

@

@

@

@

@

@

@

@

@

@

@

@

@

@

@

@

@

@

@

@

@

@

@

@

h

@

@

@

@

@

@

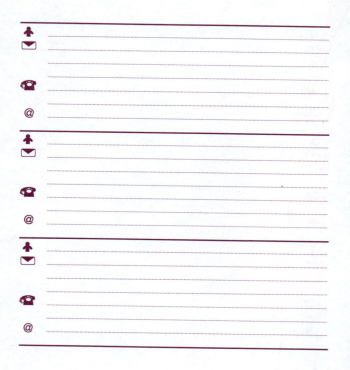

@

@

@

@

@

@

@

@

@

@

@

@

@

@

@

@

@

@

@

@

@

@

@

@

@

@

@

@

@

@

@

@

@

@

@

@

@

@

@

@

@

@

@

@

@

O

@

@

@

@

@

@

@

@

@

@

@

@

Pq

@

@

@

r

@

@

@

@

@

@

@

@

@

S

@

@

@

S

@

@

@

@

@

@

@

@

@

t

@

@

@

@

@

@

t

@

@

@

@

@

@

@

@

@

@

@

@

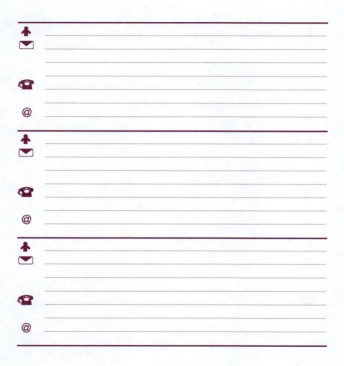

@

@

@

@

@

@

@

@

@